# A CONCISE BIOGRAPHICAL SKETCH

*the notebook edition*

Colour the Classics

xoxo

For You
xoxo

# The End

Follow us:

@colourtheclassics

www.ingramcontent.com/pod-product-compliance
Lightning Source LLC
Chambersburg PA
CBHW080856160726
47999CB00009B/3145
*9798348109325*